D1521647

Strength does not come from physical capacity.
It comes from an indomitable will.

-Ghandi

I am safe

The coloring book for meditating simply and anywhere you are.

Preface

When all the layers start to peel, what's left inside is you. This book is for you, to aid you in the process of remembering who you are. This book, nonetheless, is not made so you become a 'better version of yourself' or to improve what may seem as a 'fault', but for you to shine beyond all the imagined illusions, so you can find the core of your foundational truth.

The human being is a complex being, but also a simple one. Our lives are lived in individual terms and yet lived through collectively, the stories and narratives we carry within ourselves are repeated and circulated in a societal level and yet they are imbued and internalized at a personal level. Many times and ever so often, we do not even get to choose any of these reproduced stories that are playing in our minds; these narratives may come so early in our lives or pop up so frequently in our everyday thinking, that to wash them away it requires a special power within us that seems almost impossible to tap into, even if the will is clearly there.

This book is made to accompany you through this will, by creating a space for you to find the presence and consciousness necessary to fully and completely trace into the essence of who you are. As you focus on the inner truths that resonate with you, and which therefore, have brought you to this book, you will begin to grasp, validate and embody your core which exists above any illusion and beyond any layers that are of no use to you anymore.

The Coloring Method

In this book you will be using simple coloring exercises for meditative practices based on the *Coloring Method*. This method will be employed as a tool to incorporate your affirmation and intention by synchronizing your breath, thought, and action in coloring one single point.

This form of single-point concentration is called *samadhi* in eastern philosophical thought. In this book, you will be using samadhi, or single-point concentration, in order to place your energy and focus on the resonating point you chose on this book, the same point and mantra that you will be manifesting within you.

The *Coloring Method* follows a simple three-step process of:

Breath. Thought. and Action.

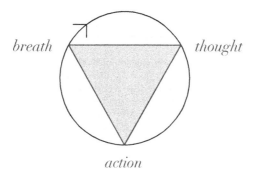

Instructions

The suggested instructions are as follows: through the **coloring** of a small circle you will be using your **breath** and **thought** to focus on manifesting your intention through action. Throughout your practice, this three-step process will start to come and flow naturally as you intuitively enter a meditative state of focused attention.

On this journey:

You will use your breath to find presence.

You will use your thoughts to embody your message.

And you will use the act coloring to energize your message.

Breath and Presence

The act of breathing constantly brings life into the body, energizing every cell with oxygen, the basis of life. For this reason, when one brings awareness to the life force, one brings awareness to presence and life.

In the following *Coloring Method* exercises you will be able to use your breath as a vehicle to bring consciousness into the now; concentrating on your breath will allow to tune into your body and into your presence.

Bringing consciousness into your breath is just as simple as bringing awareness to your inhalation and exhalation. In the next page you will find a simple breathing exercise to connect with your breath so you can start to bring awareness to this wonderful and self-sufficient mindfulness tool.

Sit in a comfortable and quiet space, and close your eyes. Begin to listen to your breath, without any need to control it or judge it, just let it be. Once you are in touch with your breathing cycle start to feel how it manifest physically in your body. When you inhale feel how your abdomen expands as you breath in, and then on an exhale feel how your abdomen deflates as it let goes of all the air inside. To get more in touch with how this process happens, you can place the palm of your hand on your abdominal region and feel your body inhaling as it expands and exhaling as the belly slowly empties the air out. Do this for a couple of minutes and feel how it feels to be with your breath.

Once you have tried this simple breathing exercise, you can bring this practice into any active meditation method, by synchronizing your breath with your movement. In the coloring method, you will be doing this by inhaling slowly and exhaling slowly as you color the dot below and repeat your mantra or affirmation.

Repeat this *breath.thought.action* technique as many times as you need to until you are done with coloring the circle and then move to the next circle. You can follow this simple three-point process of: *breath, thought, and action*, every time you color a circle.

While doing this exercise simply concentrate on your breath, your intention and coloring while you bring awareness into your body. The point is to feel present within yourself, while maintaining your awareness in the moment and in your mantra.

On the Power of Breathing

Breathing is of key importance to any meditation practice; this is the case since the way that you breath has an overall effect on the functioning of your body and your mind. The depth, frequency, and speed of your breath affects the amount of oxygen that flows into your body and into your brain. Your breath has the power to affect your heart rate, your nervous system, and the whole functioning of your body[1]. The overall breath behavior of a person is a learned behavior that carries deep ingrained habits or breathing patterns that from an early age can shape how the person experiences the world. Hence, the more conscious you are of your breath, the more control you can have on how the air flows in and out the body and in how you feel and react to the stimuli around you.

1. The phsyiological effects of slow breathing in healthy humans. Russo, Santarelli, O'rourke. 2017.

On the Power of Thoughts

The complex interrelation or looping system between the mind and the body is called the mind-body connection and it explains why it is not possible to fully comprehend thoughts without understanding the communication between all the systems in the body. Thoughts, attitudes and feelings carry the power of changing the health of your body since the brain, the nervous system, the endocrine and the immune system are in constant communication with each other[2]. Hence, how you think and feel can have a direct reaction in your physical state of being and vice versa. Understanding this simple fact can aid you in bringing power into the unforeseen force of words and thoughts.

2. Thoughts, Neurotransmitters, Body-Mind Connection. Steinberg. Psychology Today.

On the Power of Coloring and Single Point Concentration

Coloring creates an environment where mindfulness can thrive. Coloring has been proven to have the ability to help you ease into a calm mental state by facilitating a conscious state of presence through a single focused activity[3]. Coloring itself can allow your brain to focus on one task as it engages both the mind and the body in one single task. Coloring can help youhone you motor skills by allowing you to reconnect with your body and your personal expression[4]. Coloring relaxes the mind by simultaneously giving it a task and at the same time allowing it to just flow.

3. Health Benefits of Coloring for Adults. Beaumont Health System. 2016.
4. Three Reasons Adult Coloring Can Actually Relax Your Brain. Cleveland Clinic. 2015.

On the Power of
Journaling + Positive Affirmations

Positive affirmations are not about suppressing reality nor about using a mask to cover up what's "really underneath"- on the contrary, positive affirmations are powerful assertions that are meant to open up a dialogue with the experience of embodying the ancestral and everlasting universal question of Who Am I?

To affirm a positive thought is to hold a precious space for your inner wisdom to speak. Journaling facilitates this space, as it gives a platform to the thoughts that have so much to say, but that many times can feel shy or fearful to speak through other avenues.

Connecting with a positive affirmation allows you to open up a dialogue with the deepest parts of yourself. This dialogue reveals something akin to a box of treasures, treasures that hold answers and foresight into the thoughts, ideas, and memories that hold the structure of who you are. Hence, to consciously know, explore, and embody the conversations that pop up during inner-work makes all the difference.

When an inner dialogue unfolds, for the most part, we are by default, not always present with it. Thought patterns are so part of us that we naturally become engaged with them without much awareness or distance from them. As previously noted, many times dialogues can go on for years without us ever being conscious of the tape that's playing, unknowingly carrying a feeling or a persona that's being embodied through these dialogues.

Now, when it comes to asserting positive affirmations, the dialogue that's playing becomes ever present and ever clear, giving one the opportunity to listen, to what's really happening inside. For this reason, in the exercises in this book, you will be working both through repetitive coloring exercises and journaling to make the best out of your affirmation inner-work.

Know + Explore + Embody
Your Affirmation Through
Coloring and Journaling

Each *coloring meditation page* comes affixed with a *journal section* where you will be able to explore your affirmation by using a series of questions that will support your inner journey. In this way, you will be using coloring as a meditative practice by combining breath and the arts of contemplation; and then additionally you will be shinning light into your inner space with the aid of the appending journal section.

The questions from the journal section have been divided into three sections. The first set of questions deal with getting to *know your affirmation* by guiding you to inquire your relationship to it. The second part of the inner journey takes you to *explore the affirmation* by means of investigating how your identity relates to your chosen affirmation. The final and third part of the journal section takes you through *embodying your mantra* by incorporating and personifying your chosen message through the actualization of the affirmation.

Bringing attention to the dialogue that surfaces during your meditation will support you by giving space for your inner wisdom to speak. The journal questions found in this book can be used as both guides for your meditation or as sub-sequential reflection.

Final Thoughts

This book is designed for both beginner and experienced meditators alike as the following active meditation exercises are easy to engage with, and can be done anywhere and at any time.

Active meditation is a practice that includes both breathing exercises and physical movement in order to reach a state of calm, presence and clarity. This form of meditation offers many advantages in comparison with other passive techniques, such as seating meditation, since it is easier for the mind to quiet down when there is movement involved.

When meditating leave aside any judgements or expectations; a meditation session is neither good or bad, since the key to a rewarding mediation is enjoying the present moment. As you start to engage in this practice more and more, the beauty of the different experiences will surface, just as the ocean is beautifully different on every single day of the year. Sometimes a meditation practice can bring something up and sometimes it can be there, as it is, just as a practice.

Sometimes, part of the process of meditating is encountering resistance from the mind as the mind frequently tries to look away from the now and into habitual patterns based on future or past thinking. It is indeed a normal occurrence for the mind to question, challenge or resist new mental patterns, so becoming conscious of this resistance and then accepting questions as what they are, can open a growing space for transformation to unfold.

When meditating it can be helpful to become conscious of what thoughts, questions or doubts may come up, so if it is of use to you, you can write them down in the journal pages in the book. Although it might not be for everyone, journaling can aid one in exploring if there are any blockages that are keeping one from trusting one's words. For example, if one's message is "I am beautiful" and the mind says, no way!, becoming conscious of this can shed the light into one's mental processes, honing one's ability to observe the mind.

Finally, a very important tool that might come in handy when re-peating an affirmation is to mentally recite supporting words at the end of the mantra. The following examples can illustrate this tool at work. When you are meditating on a mantra, such as 'I am balanced', you can finish the mantra by saying 'I am balanced and it's ok'. This can help you to deal with doubts in a healthy way. Another way of reasserting the mantra is by giving the mantra more power; this can be done as in this example; when you are meditating on the mantra 'I am perfect' you can say 'I am perfect just as I am'.

These assertions can be very helpful when there is fear or doubt entering your thoughts as it can serve as a reminder that it is fine to be in a state of ease. Finding the words and thoughts that support you, can allow you to create supportive mental mechanisms which can become part of your support system that will always be there whenever you need it. In this way you can grant your words power and let them be your allies.

Through the use of simple mindfulness tools based on meditation practices and neuroplasticity findings on the power of meditation[5], the following pages are set to empower you in rewiring your neural network through the use breath, thought, and action.

Have the confidence that as you start to shed old habitual thought patterns there will be more space created for new mental and emotional bridges to arise in your mind and in your life. Believe, once again, that with your conscious will, you will be able to engage your energy in sowing the seeds that will grow into your own nourished field.

1. Buddha's Brain: Neuroplasticity and Meditation. Davidson and Lutz. 2008

Every time you color a circle
feel the message in your body
feel its sensations, its taste, its energy.

Embody the message by feeling it
in the crown of your head, heart,
and all the way down to your toes
and welcome this message unto you.

I am safe

I am safe & I embody this message

Know

Get to know your affirmation by
inquiring your relationship to it.

I am safe & I embody this message

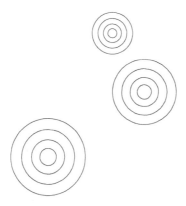

I am safe & I embody this message

Journal

write your reflections on this page

How does it feel to meet and be with with this affirmation?

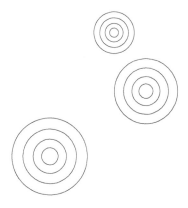

I am safe & I embody this message

Journal

What emotions or thoughts come up when you are
working with this affirmation?

I am safe & I embody this message

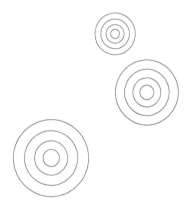

I am safe & I embody this message

Journal

How does it feel to bring presence to your affirmation
and the feelings that arise?

I am safe & I embody this message

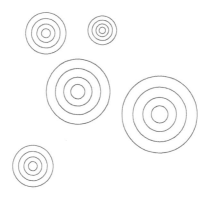

I am safe & I embody this message

Journal

Bring to mind one of the primary emotions that come up during your meditation and write how it feels to have this emotion during the meditation.

I am safe & I embody this message

Journal

What are the sensations that come up when you repeat this affirmation?
Is there a certain part of your body that feels very connected with this
affirmation? Explore this space.

I am safe & I embody this message

Journal

What are the sensations that come up when you repeat this affirmation?
Is there a certain part of your body that feels very connected with this
affirmation? Explore this space.

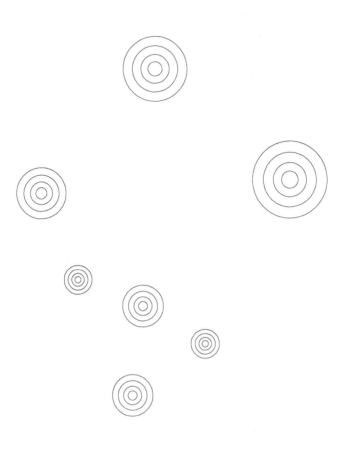

I am safe & I embody this message

Journal

What brought you to this affirmation? In this journal entry take time to explore what made you gravitate towards this affirmation.

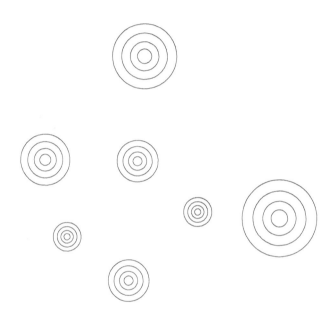

I am safe & I embody this message

Journal

Why does this affirmation hold importance to you?
Why does it resonate with you?

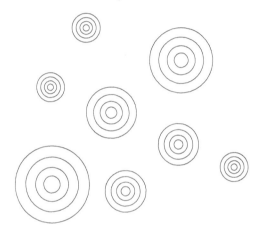

I am safe & I embody this message

Journal

Are there any questions that come up when you are practicing the meditation? What kind of questions are they? Where do they come from? how to you react to these questions?

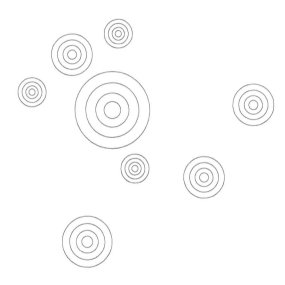

I am safe & I embody this message

Journal

Who is the inner voice that is repeating the affirmation?
How does it sound like? What is its character? What agenda does it have?

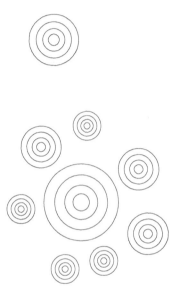

I am safe & I embody this message

Journal

Is there a voice that is speaking or responding to the voice that is repeating the affirmation? Does this voice remind you of someone? If you could talk to it what would it say?

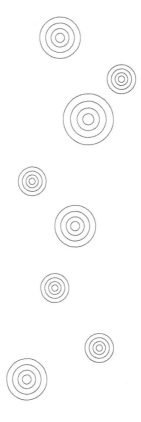

I am safe & I embody this message

Journal

Who is your inner listener that is listening to this affirmation?
How does it look like? How does it talk? What is it looking for?

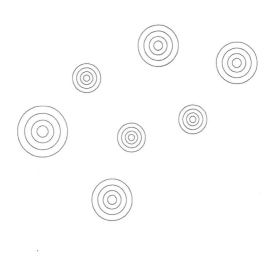

I am safe & I embody this message

Journal

Is there anything you feel like doing when you repeat this affirmation?
How does this affirmation stimulate you?

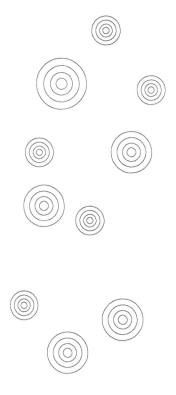

I am safe & I embody this message

Journal

How does the color you chose relate to your affirmation?
What does it symbolize? What does it mean to you?

I am safe & I embody this message

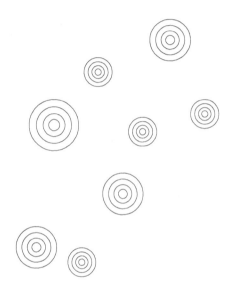

I am safe & I embody this message

Journal

What does your logical mind think about this affirmation?
If you could talk to it what would you say to it?

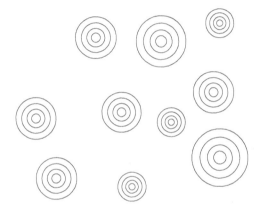

I am safe & I embody this message

Journal

How does your emotional body feel about this affirmation?
You can get in touch with your emotional body, by asking it how it feels, and
by putting your hand in your heart and taking a couple of big breaths

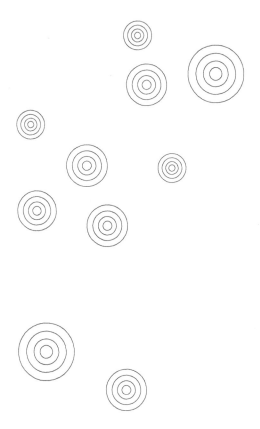

I am safe & I embody this message

Journal

How does your whole being feel and relates to this affirmation?

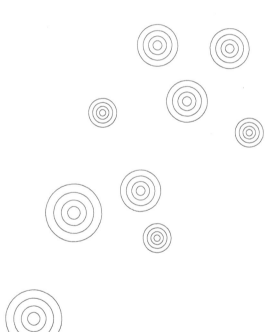

I am safe & I embody this message

Journal

How does it feel to bring this affirmation unto life?

I am safe & I embody this message

Explore

explore your affirmation by investigating
its relation to your identity.

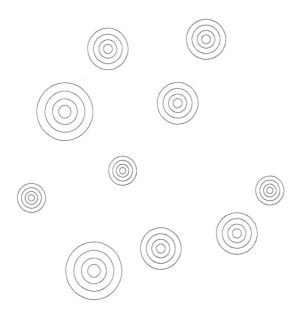

I am safe & I embody this message

Journal

What is your relation to this affirmation?
Are there any memories attached to it?

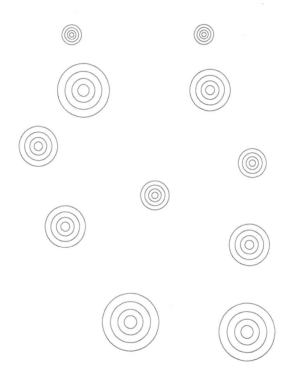

I am safe & I embody this message

Journal

Are there any images attached with this affirmation?
Stay with them for a moment and write them down.
Reflect on how you feel about them.

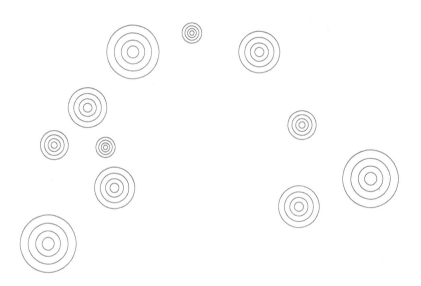

I am safe & I embody this message

Journal

Are there any narratives that keep on coming up as you work through your meditation? Write them down and when they first appeared in your life.

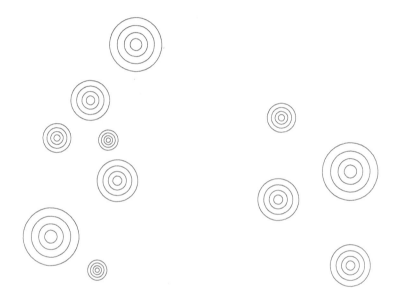

I am safe & I embody this message

Journal

Is there anything you will like to release or let go of during this meditation?

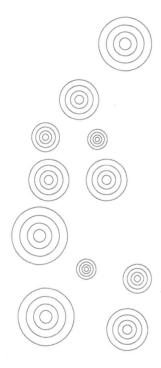

I am safe & I embody this message

Journal

How is this affirmation related to your present identity?
How can you bring this affirmation to co-exist with how you see yourself?

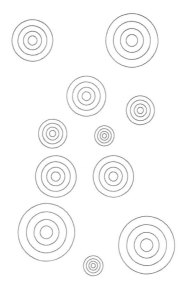

I am safe & I embody this message

Journal

How is this affirmation related to your childhood identity?
How is this affirmation related to your family dynamics?

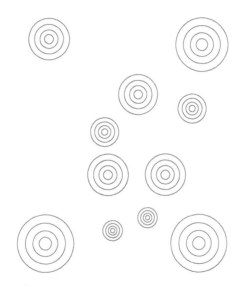

I am safe & I embody this message

Journal

How is this affirmation related to how you see your future self?
Are there any feelings that come up when you explore this?

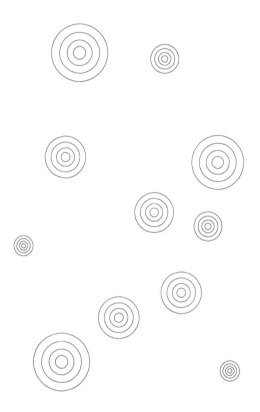

I am safe & I embody this message

Journal

How is this affirmation related to the decisions that you make?

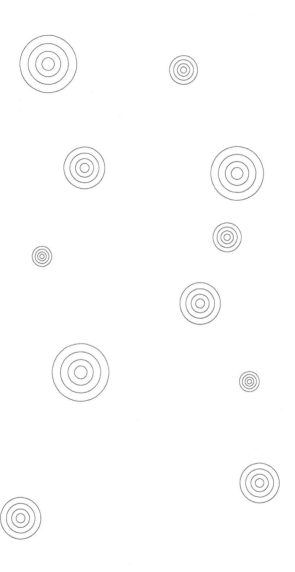

I am safe & I embody this message

Journal

Do you find yourself resisting or openly receiving this affirmation? if so, why?

I am safe & I embody this message

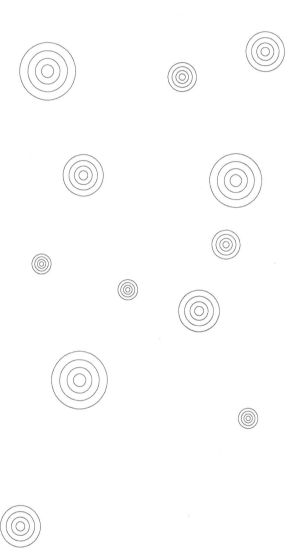

I am safe & I embody this message

Journal

Are there any specific blockages you would like to explore from this affirmation?

I am safe & I embody this message

Embody

Embody your affirmation by
incorporating your chosen message

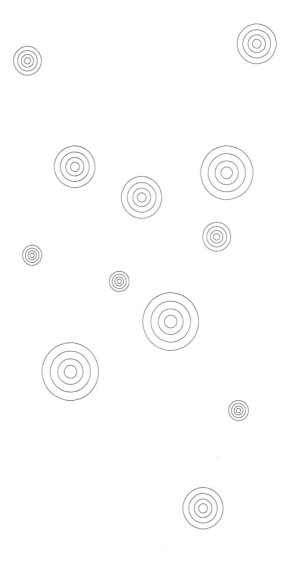

I am safe & I embody this message

Journal

How would it feel if this affirmation held absolutely true?

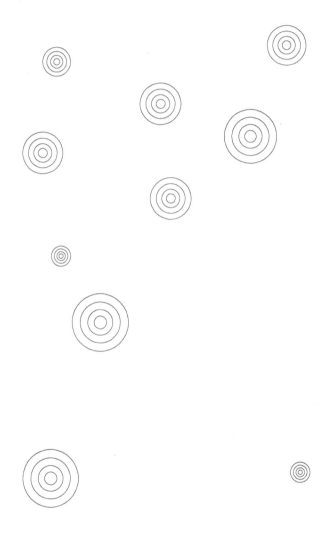

I am safe & I embody this message

Journal

How would reality feel if this affirmation was a fact?
How would you personify this affirmation?

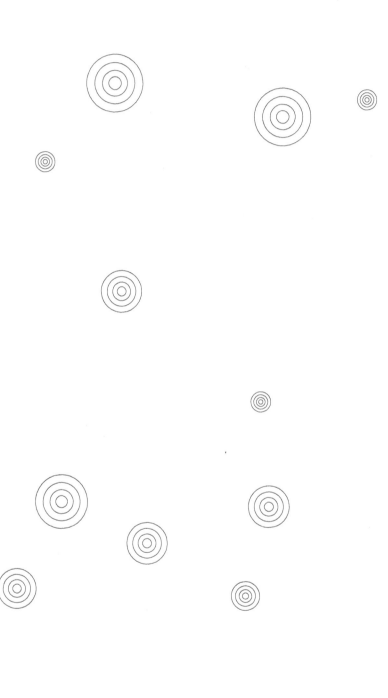

I am safe & I embody this message

Journal

How would the world feel and its sensory input
if this affirmation held fully true?

I am safe & I embody this message

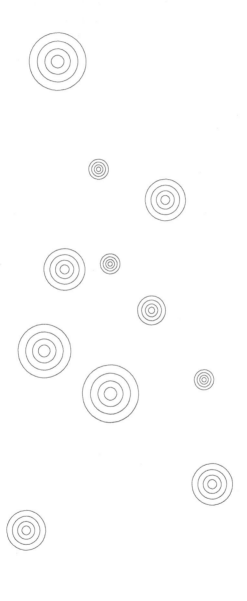

I am safe & I embody this message

Journal

How would your relationships feel if you personified this affirmation?

I am safe & I embody this message

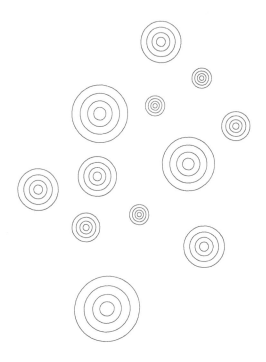

I am safe & I embody this message

Journal

How would you breathe if you embodied this affirmation ?
Take a couple of breaths then write your reflections down.

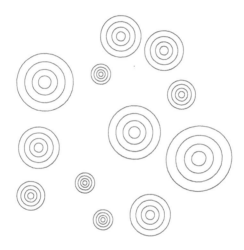

I am safe & I embody this message

Journal

How would you speak if you embodied this affirmation?

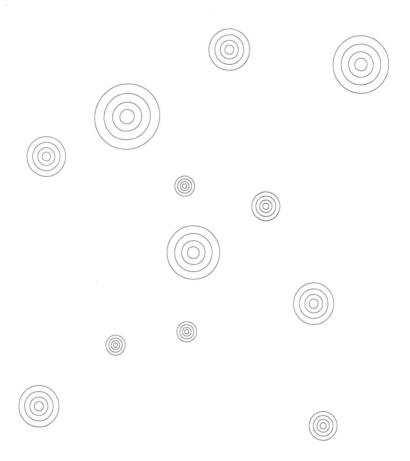

I am safe & I embody this message

Journal

How would you stand if you embodied this affirmation?

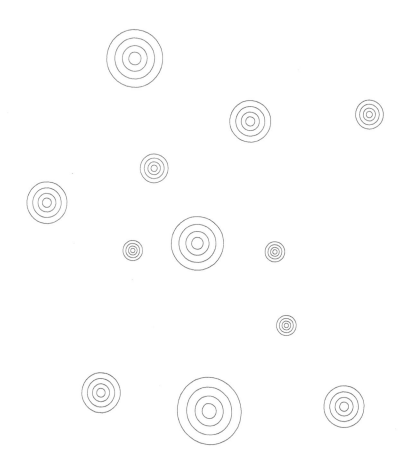

I am safe & I embody this message

Journal

How would you sit and lounge if you embodied this affirmation?

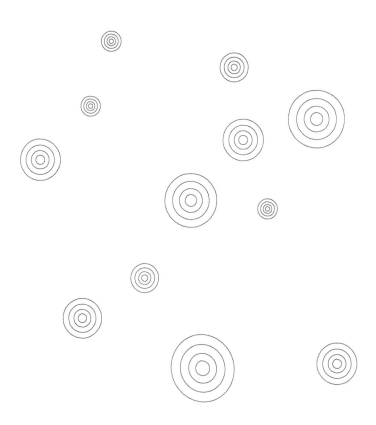

I am safe & I embody this message

Journal

How would you walk if you embodied this affirmation?

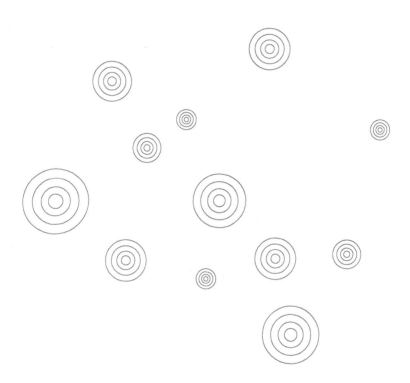

I am safe & I embody this message

Journal

How would you move if you embodied this affirmation?
How would you own your space through this affirmation?

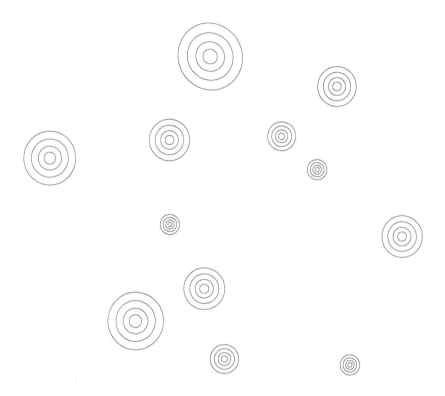

I am safe & I embody this message

Journal

How would you see the world and meet other's eyes
if you embodied this affirmation?

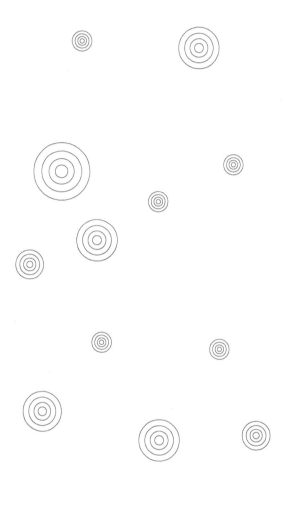

I am safe & I embody this message

Journal

How would you dance and connect with your sacred self
if you embodied this affirmation?

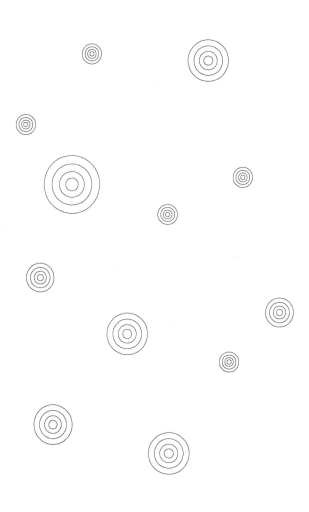

I am safe & I embody this message

Journal

How would you wake up and take on the day if you embodied this affirmation?

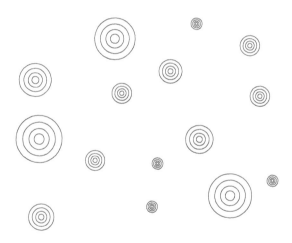

I am safe & I embody this message

Journal

How would you go to sleep and relax if you embodied this affirmation?

I am safe & I embody this message

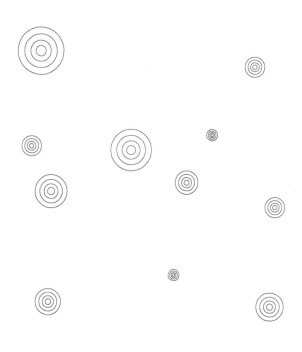

I am safe & I embody this message

Journal

How would you sing and speak if you embodied this affirmation?

I am safe & I embody this message

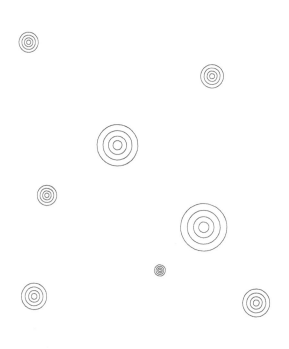

I am safe & I embody this message

Journal

How would you smile and laugh if you embodied this affirmation?

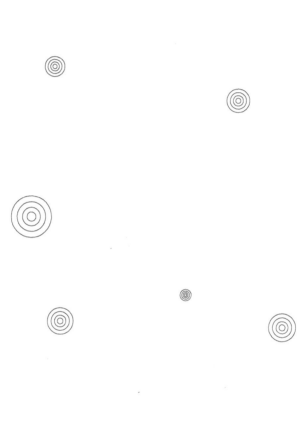

I am safe & I embody this message

Journal

How would it taste like if you embodied this affirmation?
How would life taste like?

I am safe & I embody this message

Journal

How would the body fully feel if this affirmation was your core truth?

I am safe & I embody this message

Journal

(write your own reflection)

I am safe & I embody this message

Acknowledgements

Thanks to Rune for his unlimited support and love. Thanks to my dog Amelie, whose soul always shines through her heart and her eyes. Thanks to Lindita and Sarah, my wonderful yoga teachers who saw so much life in me and validated this simple truth through their presence and support. And thanks to Floriana, for making me see that I'm much more than my fears, for making me see, once again, the beauty in me. May all the blessings be with you.

More Book Titles and Series

I AM SERIES

I am beautiful

I am balanced

I am present

I am complete

I am calm

I am confident

I am connected

I am courageous

I am loved

I am loving

I am kind

I am good

I am amazing

I am grounded

I am conscious

I am wonderful

I am trust

I am focused

I am independent

I am wise

I am healthy

I am strong

I am brave

I am clarity

I am nourishment

I am the path

I am thankful

I am free

I am power

I am me

I am perfect

I am aware

I am here

I am safe

I am peace

I am relaxed

I am alive

I am fulfilled

I am sincere

I am life

THERE IS SERIES

There is peace

There is love

There is understanding

There is connection

There is collaboration

There is hope

There is reason

There is sense

There is listening

There is time

There is space

There is meaning

There is genuineness

There is silence

There is life

There is wisdom

There is consciousness

SPIRITUAL SERIES

I am sacred

I am human

I am flow

I am nature

I am light

I am awakened

I believe

I belong

I am love

I am centered

I am aligned

I am flow

I have flow

I am warmness

I am there

I am breath

I am healed

I am life

I am sustenance

I am the journey

I am connected

I am magic

I am energy

YOGA MANTRA SERIES

Om

Om Shanti

Om Namah Shivaya

Chakras

Made in USA - North Chelmsford, MA
1097612_9781793858269
05.04.2020 2024